Facing New Horizons Through
Active Children's Programs
LSCA Title I Grant
1987

Giant Water Bugs

This book has been reviewed
for accuracy by
Walter L. Gojmerac
Professor of Entomology
University of Wisconsin—Madison.

Library of Congress Cataloging in Publication Data

Pohl, Kathleen.
    Giant water bugs.

    (Nature close-ups)
    Adaptation of: Kooimushi / Jun Nanao and
Hidetomo Oda.
    Summary: Describes in text and photographs the
physical characteristics, life cycle, and behavior
of giant water bugs.
    1. Belastomatidae—Juvenile literature.
[1. Water bugs]   I. Nanao, Jun. Kooimushi.
II. Title.   III. Series.
QL523.B4P64   1986   595.7'54   86-28016
ISBN 0-8172-2714-8 (lib. bdg.)
ISBN 0-8172-2732-6 (softcover)

This edition first published in 1987 by Raintree Publishers Inc.

Text copyright © 1987 by Raintree Publishers Inc., translated by
Jun Amano from *Giant Water Bug* copyright © 1976 by Jun Nanao and
Hidetomo Oda.

Photographs copyright © 1976 by Hidekazu Kubo.

World English translation rights for *Color Photo Books on Nature*
arranged with Kaisei-Sha through Japan Foreign-Rights Center.

1 2 3 4 5 6 7 8 9 0   90 89 88 87 86

Giant Water Bugs

Adapted by
Kathleen Pohl

Raintree Publishers
Milwaukee

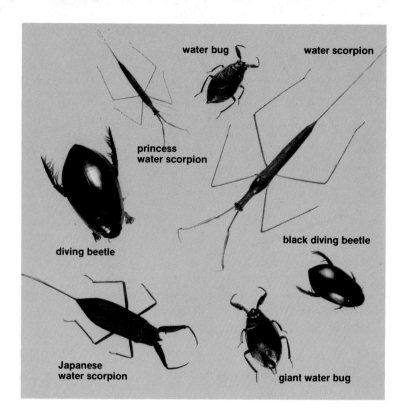

water bug

water scorpion

princess
water scorpion

diving beetle

black diving beetle

Japanese
water scorpion

giant water bug

◄ **Different kinds of underwater insects.**

Diving beetles are among the biggest of the water beetles. Some are almost three inches long. Both diving beetles and giant water bugs are fierce underwater hunters. Long-legged water scorpions look like a cross between a walking stick and a praying mantis.

▶ **Someone collecting pond insects in winter.**

Many kinds of insects live the year-round in freshwater lakes and ponds. If you were to break through a layer of ice on the pond's surface on an early spring day, you would find a variety of insects. Many would be beetles of one sort or another—whirligig beetles, water scavengers, and diving beetles.

Many others would be what scientists call "true bugs." Among them are backswimmers and water boatmen. As their name suggests, backswimmers swim upside down on their backs in the water. Water boatmen use their oarlike legs to "row" themselves through the water. Other true bugs include the long-legged water striders, water scorpions, and giant water bugs.

Giant water bugs are oval-shaped and are brownish in color. They are among the largest of all insects— some measure four or five inches long. Most giant water bugs live in tropical countries, although some can be found in the United States. Giant water bugs are sometimes called "electric light bugs" because they are attracted to outdoor lights that shine in the night.

Giant water bugs are fierce underwater hunters, or predators. They hide among the waterweeds near the bottom of lakes and ponds and wait for small fish, tadpoles, or other insects to swim by. Then the water bug reaches out with its two front legs to seize its prey. The legs are shaped like tongs and have sharp hooks which enable the water bug to catch animals that are larger than itself—frogs, toads, salamanders, and even small snakes.

▶ **A giant water bug watching small fish swim by.**

This water bug is well hidden as it waits for prey because its color blends with the color of the tree branch.

▲ **A school of killifish swimming in a pond in spring.**

▼ A giant water bug sucking the body fluids of a fish.

The water bug seizes its prey with its two hooked front legs, then uses its proboscis to inject it with poison.

▶ **A shield bug sucking plant sap.**

▶ **A shield bug sucking plant sap.**
This shield bug uses its long proboscis to suck plant sap and flower nectar. On this same plant are eggs laid by the shield bug.

All true bugs have sucking mouthparts. Once the giant water bug has grasped a small fish or other prey, it pierces it with its sharp, beaklike mouth, called a proboscis. Then the giant water bug injects a poison into its victim. The poison paralyzes the prey. The giant water bug begins to eat its dinner—it sucks the body fluids of its victim.

Not all true bugs are predators. Some, like the shield bug, use their mouthparts to suck sap from plants and pollen and nectar from flowers.

There are many families of true bugs. Each family has different traits, or characteristics. Scientists put giant water bugs in the Belastomatidae family. Shield bugs belong to a different family, the Pentatomidae family.

◀ **A Japanese water scorpion (left) and a water scorpion (right).**

The colors and shapes of their bodies help keep these water scorpions well hidden as they wait for insects, small fish, and other prey to swim near.

▶ **A giant water bug sticking its breathing tube out of the water.**

The water bug's breathing tube is much shorter than the water scorpion's. Both insects can store oxygen and take it with them underwater. The adult giant water bug stores oxygen beneath its wings and in its midsection, or thorax.

Water scorpions belong to the Nepidae family. Like giant water bugs, water scorpions are predators. These stick-like insects crawl slowly along the pond's bottom, or hide on underwater branches and leaves, and wait for small animals to swim by. They use their long, hooked front legs to seize their prey. Then the water scorpion pierces its victim with its needle-like proboscis and sucks its body fluids.

Giant water bugs, water scorpions, and other pond insects need oxygen to breathe, or they would die. Water bugs have short tubes at the tip of the abdomen, the back part of the body, for taking in oxygen from the air. Water scorpions have very long breathing tubes. They may be as long as the rest of the insect's body. Both water scorpions and giant water bugs go to the water's surface from time to time and stick their breathing tubes above the water to take in oxygen. Both insects store oxygen and take it with them so that they can breathe underwater.

Most adult water insects mate in the spring of the year, in the same pond or lake that they hibernated in during the winter.

Most water insects spend the winter hibernating, or resting, near the bottom of a pond or lake. But as the water warms up in the spring, the insects become active again. They begin to search for food, and they look for mates, and for places to lay their eggs.

Once a male and female water scorpion have mated, the male soon dies.

The female leaves the water to lay her eggs. She searches for moss, or soft, decaying plants, which make good nest sites for her eggs. The newly laid water scorpion eggs are funny looking. Long, slender breathing tubes extend from them. Each egg has two to nine tubes, depending on the kind, or species, of water scorpion.

▲ **A swamp in spring.**

Water scorpions come out of the water to lay their eggs in the spring. The eggs are kept moist by warm spring rains.

▶ **Japanese water scorpion eggs.**

The eggs are laid out of water so that they will be able to breathe. If the breathing tubes become covered with water, the eggs cannot breathe and they will die.

● Water scorpion nymphs emerging from the egg cases.

As the nymphs emerge from the eggs, they stretch their long bodies. Soon they return to the water and begin to hunt for food.

Insects go through definite physical changes as they develop. They are said to go through a metamorphosis. The word *metamorphosis* means "change." Some insects, like water scorpions and giant water bugs, go through three stages: egg, nymph, and adult. Because the nymphs are very similar to the adult insects, scientists call this an incomplete metamorphosis. Other insects go through four definite stages: egg, larva, pupa, and adult. At the larval stage, the developing insect looks very different from the adult. Scientists call this a complete metamorphosis.

As the water scorpion nymph develops inside the egg case, it breathes oxygen through the breathing tubes. It takes about two weeks for this species of water scorpion nymph to come out of, or emerge from, the egg case. When the tiny nymph emerges, it looks very much like an adult water scorpion, except that it is paler in color and does not yet have wings.

▶ A water scorpion nymph in the water.

◀ **A giant water bug eating a snail.**

Because it can paralyze its victims, the giant water bug is able to eat prey larger than itself—snails, frogs, and small fish.

▶ **A male giant water bug carrying eggs on his back.**

Although the male may be unwilling at first, he still turns out to be one of the best babysitters in the insect world.

Giant water bugs do not leave the water to lay their eggs. The females of many species lay their eggs in clusters on plants that grow in the water. The females of a few species lay their eggs on the backs of male giant water bugs. The male is not a willing father at first. He may try to fight off the female, but she is larger than he is and can overpower him. She seizes him between her front legs and forces him to stay still. Then she plasters his back with a glue-like substance and lays her eggs. She may lay 150 to 175 eggs at a time. The eggs remain glued to the male giant water bug's back as he moves about in the water.

◄ A male giant water bug attracting a female.

If a female giant water bug has not laid many eggs on the male's back, he may shake his body to attract another female to him. Then the two giant water bugs mate.

▶ A female giant water bug laying her eggs.

While the male stays still on a dead branch or water plant, the female lays her eggs, one by one, on his back. The eggs measure about one-tenth of an inch long.

If a male giant water bug is not carrying many eggs on his back, he may shake his body to attract another female. As soon as the two insects mate, the female lays her eggs on the male's back.

The female giant water bug may have to find two or three males to carry all her eggs. Or, she may wait until the first batch of eggs hatches. Then she carefully removes the empty eggshells from the male's back and lays more eggs.

◀ **A male water bug carrying many eggs.**

The giant water bug carries the eggs with him to warm, shallow water. He floats on the surface so the eggs can absorb fresh oxygen from the air.

▶ **A male giant water bug that has just caught something to eat.**

Male giant water bugs do not swim around much while they are babysitting the eggs. But if an insect or small fish swims near, the giant water bug will reach out with his hooked front legs to seize his prey.

Inside the egg cases, tiny water bug nymphs are developing. The male giant water bug knows instinctively how to care for them. He swims to the warm shallows of the lake or pond to keep the eggs warm. He swims often to the water's surface because the eggs need oxygen to breathe.

Because the eggs are white, they can be seen easily by birds and other predators. If the male giant water bug senses danger, he dives quickly into the water to flee from enemies.

The male giant water bug continues his babysitting duties until the eggs are ready to hatch.

As the bodies of the nymphs form inside the eggs, their black eyes become visible through the egg cases. By the time the nymphs are ready to emerge from the eggs, they have developed sharp, needlelike mouths and strong front legs. It takes just a few days for the nymphs of some species of giant water bugs to develop. Other species may take as long as two weeks to develop fully.

The male giant water bug seems to sense when the eggs are ready to hatch. He swims to the surface of the lake or pond. As soon as the eggs are exposed to the air, they begin to hatch.

▼ The eyes of nymphs can be seen through the egg cases.

▶ A giant water bug nymph beginning to emerge.

The male giant water bug swims to the water's surface when the eggs are ready to hatch.

● **The birth of a giant water bug nymph.**

The giant water bug nymph slowly pushes its way out of the egg case. It rests for a short time, then begins to float in the water.

The nymphs break through the top of the egg cases, slowly stretching out their bodies. They have large black eyes and tiny bodies that are pale in color. The nymphs look very much like adult giant water bugs except that they are much smaller and lighter in color. And they do not yet have wings.

The newly emerged nymphs cling to the male giant water bug's back. They breathe in oxygen from the air. Then the giant water bug dips slowly into the water and the nymphs begin to float on their own. At first, they live in shallow water, clinging to the stalks of waterweeds. As they grow larger and become more developed, they move to deeper waters where other adult giant water bugs live.

◀ **A giant water bug that has molted for the last time.**

After the last molting, the giant water bug has soft, white wings. The two pairs of wings soon harden and darken in color.

Adult giant water bugs can use their wings to fly from pond to pond.

Giant water bug nymphs are able to survive on their own as soon as they are born. The nymphs use their hooked front legs to catch water insects and other prey. They eat a good deal and their bodies grow rapidly.

But the nymph's hard outer skin does not grow, so the nymph must molt, or shed its skin, as it gets bigger. The number of times the nymph molts depends on the species of water bug. The species shown in these pictures molts five times before it becomes an adult. With its last molt, it gets two pairs of wings. They are soft and white at first, but they soon harden and darken in color. After its last molt, the giant water bug's metamorphosis is complete—it has become an adult.

When it was a nymph, the giant water bug lived in shallow water because it couldn't store and carry very much oxygen. The oxygen it did store was kept in a sac in the abdomen. But the adult giant water bug can store greater amounts of oxygen beneath its wings, and is able to live in the deeper waters of a lake or pond.

▼ **A giant water bug swimming.** The two back pairs of legs are used like oars as the giant water bug paddles through the water.

The adult giant water bug is a good swimmer. Its flat, wide body moves easily through the water. Its two pairs of powerful hind legs are covered with tiny hairs. These help to propel the insect quickly through the water.

Giant water bugs have two pairs of wings and are good fliers. When giant water bugs are flying, they breathe through openings called spiracles. These are located on the thorax, or midsection, of the body.

By autumn, a pond may become overcrowded with insects. Many different kinds of adult water insects have been mating and reproducing all summer. Diving beetle larvae, dragonfly nymphs, water scorpion nymphs, and other developing insects are all hunting for food in the same pond. If a pond becomes too crowded, or if food becomes scarce, adult giant water bugs may leave the pond and fly to another, less crowded, one.

◀ **Insects in a pond in autumn.**

Water scorpions (top) and diving beetles (middle) may move from the shallow part of a pond to deeper water in the fall. The funny-looking creature half buried in the silt at the pond's bottom is a dragonfly nymph (lower).

▶ **A giant water bug attacking a dragonfly nymph.**

This giant water bug uses its hooked front legs to seize its prey. Then it stings the dragonfly nymph, paralyzing it. Finally, the water bug drinks its victim's body fluids.

▲ A giant water bug preparing for hibernation.

Some giant water bugs leave the water to hibernate beneath plant leaves.

◀ Water scorpions hibernating.

These water scorpions blend in with the dried grasses in which they are hibernating. This helps keep them hidden from enemies.

In fall, when the weather turns colder, insects begin to prepare for the winter. Many of them hibernate through the cold weather. Giant water bugs hibernate under dead leaves at the edge of lakes and ponds. Some come out of the water and hibernate beneath dried leaves on the ground around the pond.

Other types of water insects choose other places to hibernate. Water scorpions and diving beetles hibernate on the bottom of ponds, among the waterweeds growing there.

In spring, the insects that have lived through the winter awaken, hungry from their long winter's sleep. They begin to search for food and soon they will mate. And so the life cycle of the giant water bug continues.

▼ A pond with dead plant stalks and leaves.

Some plants in and around ponds die in winter. Insects hibernate during the winter beneath the dead plants.

GLOSSARY

abdomen—the back, or rear part, of an insect's body. (pp. 11, 26)

hibernation—a period of inactivity undergone by animals during cold weather when their body functions slow down. (pp. 12, 30, 31)

instinct—behavior with which an animal is born, rather than behavior which is learned. (p. 20)

metamorphosis—a process of development during which physical changes take place. Complete metamorphosis involves four stages: egg, larva, pupa, and adult. Incomplete metamorphosis occurs in three stages: egg, nymph, and adult. (pp. 14, 26)

molt—to shed the outer skin. (p. 26)

predators—animals that hunt and kill other animals for food. (pp. 6, 9)

prey—animals that are killed by predators. (pp. 6, 9, 11)

proboscis—a tubelike mouth used for sucking liquids or body fluids. (pp. 9, 11)

species—a group of animals which scientists have identified as having common traits. (pp. 12, 16)